10664010

BASIC PARKOUR

Basic Parkour and Freerunning Handbook

Survival Fitness Series

Sam Fury

Illustrations by Shumona Mallick

This publication is made with the approval and guidance of Bert Luxing, creator of the Survival Fitness Plan.

Copyright Sam Fury © 2014

www.SurvivalFitnessPlan.com/Sam-Fury-Amazon

All Rights Reserved

No part of this document may be reproduced without written consent from the author.

Warnings and Disclaimers

The information in this publication is made public for reference only.

Neither the author, publisher, nor anyone else involved in the production of this publication is responsible for how the reader uses the information or the result of his/her actions.

Consult a physician before undertaking any new form of physical activity.

Contents

Introduction

When I was a child (like many other children) I loved to climb trees, try to balance on stuff, roll on the ground, and other similar activities. The only difference is I never really grew out of it.

Imagine my happiness when I discovered Parkour as a young adult. It meant I could do all those things and when other adults asked "what the hell are you doing jumping around like a fool?" I could reply... "Parkour... it's a legit activity, like martial arts."

Now Parkour to me is so much more. It is a vital part of the Survival Fitness Plan. Imagine being chased by an attacker that may be faster than you, but because of your parkour skills you can easily out-maneuver him/her. For this kind of skill, you only need the foundations. That is why this book is only basic parkour. In the Survival Fitness Plan, functionality for survival is what counts, not flashy movements. Know the basics and drill them so they are instinctive.

Parkour is a great way to keep fit, a tremendous confidence builder, a means of expression, and a pathway to seeing your surroundings in a new light.

These are only some of the things I love about parkour. I hope you have similar experiences.

Get Your FREE Parkour Training Schedule and More at

www.SurvivalFitnessPlan.com

How to Gain Superior Balance

Balance is mostly mental. Be confident. Just stand up straight and walk as you usually would.

The line of balance in your foot runs down through the heel, along the arch and out through the second toe.

Focus on the point about a meter (3 feet) of where your feet are.

Keep your knees slightly bent.

Lower yourself when you feel unsteady.

When practicing your balance, vary the situation. Close your eyes, crouch down, vary widths, heights etc.

Quadrupedal Movement

Quadrupedal movement is moving on all four limbs. Your hands are shoulder width apart directly underneath your shoulders.

Your back and shins are roughly parallel to the ground.

Your toes touch the ground but your knees to not.

You knees stay about the same distance from the ground all the time.

To move forward, alternate arms and legs i.e. your right hand goes forward at the same time as your left leg.

Avoid stretching yourself out, bringing your knees too close to your body or sticking your bum out.

If resting, crouch. Do not put your knees on the ground.

Once comfortable, practice moving up and down stairs, on rails, sideways, backwards, get really low etc.

If you're enjoying this book so far, please leave a review.

<u>www.SurvivalFitnessPlan.com/Basic-Parkour-Review-Amazon</u>

7

The Safest Way to Land

Land so that both your feet hit the surface at the same time.

Land on the ball of your foot and then roll your heels down towards the ground.

Bend your knees as you land, but not too much.

If not continuing forward motion after the land, sink down through your feet.

Your arms/hands can be used for assistance and/or balance but not to take the impact.

Rolling

As height and speed is increased, you need to roll to absorb shock.

Stand with one foot a natural step in front of the other, shoulder width apart.

Your lead foot i.e. the one forward most, is on the same side as the shoulder you wish to roll over.

Crouch down.

Place your hands in line with your rear foot.

Your rear side hand is forward most and facing forward.

Your other hand points 90° from the direction you are rolling in.

Lower your lead forearm to the ground and keep it on the inside of the same side leg.

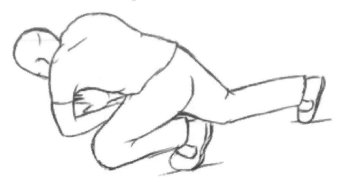

Push with your back leg to roll over your arm and onto your shoulder.

As the back of your shoulder makes contact with the ground tuck your heel to your backside.

Roll in a diagonal across your back, from your shoulder to your hip, and then onto your feet.

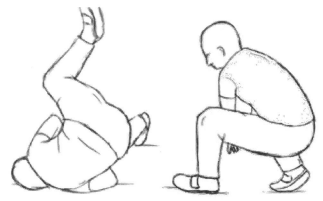

As height and speed increases land with your feet closer together and be more adaptable with your arms.

Also practice rolling backwards and sideways.

Jumping with Maximum Precision

This is known as the precision jump. From a standing position you will jump from one point to another.

Start with your feet together.

Get into a semi-crouch position.

Move your arms behind you and shift your weight to the balls of your feet.

Lean forward.

The greater the distance you need to jump, the greater the lean.

As you jump, throw your arms forwards and upwards.

Your energy travels up the legs, through the torso and into the hands.

Aim to arc up and then come down on to the landing area.

Once in the air, bring your heels to your backside.

Then bring your knees forward and push your feet towards the landing point.

Land using the balls of your feet, as quiet as you can. Do not stumble forward.

Jumping to a Wall

Jump towards and hang off your destination.

Once in the air, bring your knees forward straight in front of your body and your arms in front of you ready to grab the edge of the wall.

Contact the wall with your feet first, as opposed to your hands. Arc into your landing keeping your feet apart and avoid landing too high on the wall.

From here, either drop down or climb up the wall.

The Fastest Way to Climb Walls

From the hanging position, use the Climb Up to get up and/or over the wall. Whilst hanging by the hands put your feet on the wall with one foot slightly above the other.

Push your feet into the wall, not down.

Explosively pull your head and chest over the wall.

To build up your strength practice it in reverse i.e. start from the upright position and lower into the arm jump position.

Running Up High Walls

Known as the Wall Run, you are not actually running up the wall, but when done quickly and smoothly, it gives that impression. It used to climb high walls.

Jog towards the wall.

At approximately one stride away raise one leg whilst preparing to jump off the other.

Contact the wall with the ball of your foot at about the same distance up the wall as the distance your take off foot is away from the wall.

Swing your arms up as you step up and lean your upper body slightly towards the wall to redirect you up.

After the initial push you may be able to get another step or two.

The less sound you make the better.

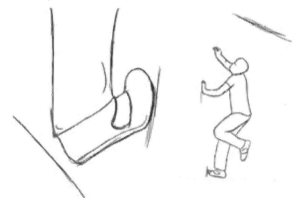

Jumping Between Walls

Use the Tic-Tac to jump from one wall to another.

Approach the wall on an angle of approximately 45°.

The higher your foot placement the more lift and distance you will achieve.

Propel yourself up with the jump off the wall to arc onto your target.

Point your chest and shoulders towards your destination.

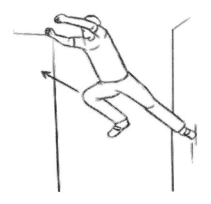

Vaults

Different obstacles utilize different techniques to overcome them. These techniques are called Passements.

Speed Vault

The Speed Vault is a general technique used to pass over medium sized obstacles quickly.

Approach the obstacle and leave the ground from your left foot (assuming you want your legs to go to the right).

Kick your right leg up to assist the body.

Reach your left arm out to make contact with the obstacle.

Your feet leave the ground before your hand makes contact.

Your hand is primarily used to for stabilization, but can also be a pivot point or an extra push for momentum.

If needed for stability, tap your outside foot on the obstacle.

As you exit drop your left foot towards the ground before your right, land upright and then continue to run.

Note: *If you are exiting on a different direction you took off from it is usually because you are 'riding' the obstacle with your arm.*

Dash Vault

The Dash Vault is used specifically when approaching obstacles front on.

Start in the same way as the Speed Vault.

As you start to pass over the obstacle bring your backside parallel to the ground and place your trailing hand on the obstacle.

Either push off with your hands or just ride the obstacle.

Land and continue running.

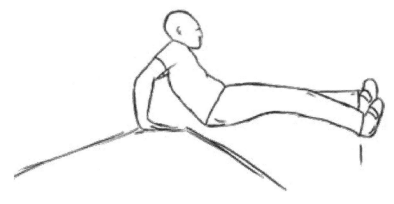

Lazy Vault

The Lazy Vault is used on obstacles that you approach at an angle.

Approach as you would for Speed Vault.

Kick up your outside leg and tuck the inside leg.

Swap your hands as you pass over the obstacle e.g. if vaulting from the right side of the body, your right hand initially makes contact with the obstacle and changes to your left as you pass over it.

Turn Vault

Use the Turn Vault if you want to stop on the other side of an obstacle.

Grasp the rail with left palm facing upwards and your right palm facing down.

Put your right leg over the rail.

Move your hips over to straddle the rail.

Support yourself with your hands keeping your bum off the rail.

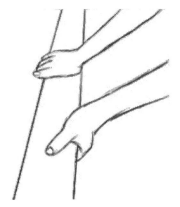

Place your right foot on the other side.

Switch your right hand to the other side of your left hand.

Cat Pass

The Cat Pass is used on high and long obstacles.

As you approach the obstacle grasp and throw it underneath yourself.

Keep your knees tucked to your chest and extend your legs to land on the other side.

Underbars

The Underbar is for passing through a vertical gap between obstacles. There are two types.

Straight Underbar

As you approach step off one foot while launching the other through the gap.

Bring your take-off foot up to the same place as the launched leg.

Reach forward and grasp the bar.

As you pull through, lay back so your upper torso and head can pass. Direct your legs upwards.

Once clear, release and run.

Reverse Underbar

Approach the rail from the side with the drop and reach forward for the bar.

If your right foot leads, cross arms with the right arm underneath the left.

Your right hand palm faces towards you and your left hand palm faces away.

Pull yourself up through the gap.

Unwind your body by pulling your chest towards the bar.

Drive your right knee up and around the body to continue to twist around.

Place your left foot on the ground and release the left hand.

Once you are facing the right way, release and run.

Bonus Freebies

Dear Reader,

Thank you for reading **Basic Parkour**. If you enjoyed it, I would really appreciate if you left a review on Amazon. www.SurvivalFitnessPlan.com/Basic-Parkour-Review-Amazon

If you have any feedback or constructive criticism, please share it with me via the SurvivalFitnessPlan contact form: www.SurvivalFitnessPlan.com/Contact

Claim your bonus freebies at:
www.SurvivalFitnessPlan.com/Book-Bonus-Freebies

Download the bonus freebies for Essential Parkour Training.

The password is: EPPFS&^45

Get FREE training schedules and more by joining our newsletter:
www.SurvivalFitnessPlan.com

Follow us for the latest book promotion deals:
www.Facebook.com/SurvivalFitnessPlan
www.Twitter.com/Survival_Fitnes

Thanks again for your support,
Sam Fury, Author.

Author Recommendations

If you enjoyed this book, you may also like:

The Survival Fitness Bundle

The Survival Fitness Bundle is a self-training manual in the 5 most useful activities for escaping danger. It includes parkour, climbing, swimming, riding, and hiking. There is also a simple daily routine to keep your mind and body in optimal health with minimal effort.

Get your copy of *The Survival Fitness Bundle* today on Kindle and/or in print.

www.SurvivalFitnessPlan.com/Survival-Fitness

Wilderness and Travel Medicine

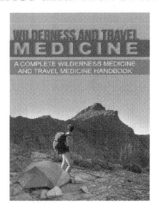

A comprehensive wilderness and travel medicine guide. Contains prevention, diagnoses, and treatments for a wide range of ailments using modern and "survival" medicines.

Get your copy of *Wilderness and Travel Medicine* today on Kindle and/or in print.

www.SurvivalFitnessPlan.com/Wilderness-Travel-Medicine

Survival Fitness Plan Training Manuals

Health and Fitness

Keep your body in optimal condition with minimal effort. The health and fitness series covers:

- **Nutrition and conditioning.** The 2 fundamentals for health and fitness.
- **Yoga.** Making Yoga a part of you daily routine will keep your mind and body healthy and in sync. Certain Yoga sequences are also a good alternative cure for many ailments.
- **Massage Therapy.** For prevention and healing of training injuries as well as general relaxation.

www.SurvivalFitnessPlan.com/Health-Fitness-Series

Survival Fitness

This series contains training manuals on the best methods of flight. Together with self-defense (fight), you can train in them for general health and fitness.

- **Parkour.** All the essential parkour skills needed to overcome obstacles in your path.
- **Climbing.** Focusing on essential bouldering techniques. Many of these skills transfer well into parkour.
- **Riding.** Essential mountain bike riding techniques. Go as fast as possible in the safest manner.
- **Swimming.** Swimming for endurance and/or speed using the most efficient strokes.

www.SurvivalFitnessPlan.com/Survival-Fitness-Series

Self-Defense

The Self-Defense Series has volumes on some of the martial arts used as a base in SFP Self-Defense. It also contains the SFP Self-Defense training manuals. SFP Self-Defense is an efficient and effective form of minimalist self-defense.

www.SurvivalFitnessPlan.com/Self-Defense-Series

Escape Evasion, and Survival

SFP escape, evasion, and survival skills (EES) focus on minimalism. It is EES using little to no special equipment.

- **Escape and Evasion.** The ability to escape capture and hide from your enemy.

- **Urban and Wilderness Survival.** Being able to live off the land in all terrains.

- **Emergency Roping.** Basic climbing skills and improvised roping techniques.

- **Water Rescue.** Life-saving water skills based on surf life-saving and military training course competencies.

- **Wilderness First Aid.** Modern medicine for use in emergency situations.

Specific subjects covered include entry and exit techniques, evasive driving, hostile negotiation tactics, lock-picking, urban survival, wilderness survival, computer hacking, and more.

www.SurvivalFitnessPlan.com/Escape-Evasion-Survival-Series

Author Bio

Sam has had an interest in self-preservation and survival for as long as he can remember. This has lead to years of training and career-related experience in related subjects.

Sam describes himself as a "Survivalist, Minimalist, Traveler". He spends his time traveling the world and refining his skills. He has studied Martial Arts with the masters in China and the Philippines. Sam has also trained with experts in parkour, survival, alternative healing, and more.

Now he shares his knowledge with the world through his books.

Follow Sam Fury

www.SurvivalFitnessPlan.com/Sam-Fury-Amazon

www.SurvivalFitnessPlan.com/Sam-Fury-Goodreads

www.SurvivalFitnessPlan.com